"I do believe in simplicity…

Simplify the problem of life,

distinguish the necessary and

the real. Probe the earth to see

where your main roots run."

Henry David Thoreau
Letter to H. G. O. Blake, March 27, 1848

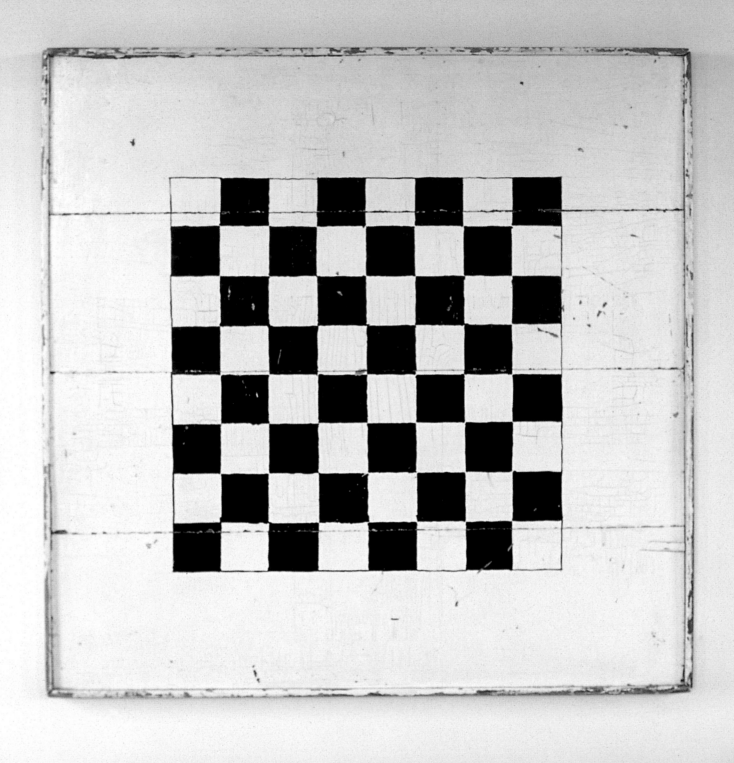

AMERICAN

COUNTRY

HERBERT
YPMA

STEWART, TABORI & CHANG

NEW YORK

PAGES 2–3
Clapboard, originally named after the sound made by lengths of planking when they hit the ground, is one of the most distinctive elements of American vernacular architecture. Owing to the abundance of timber in the New World, clapboard, usually painted "barn red," was a popular and economical choice for building barns and houses.

PAGES 4–5
The carved decoration on the timber doors of a church in Sag Harbor, built in the Greek Revival style, repeats a pattern found throughout early American craft, particularly in quilts. The shape is based on that of

"martin holes," made by farmers in the sides of barns to allow swallows and other small birds to pass through.

PAGES 6–7
This photograph of early morning mist over a pond nestled in the dunes of Long Island's famous Hamptons attests to the beauty that has attracted settlers, pioneers, farmers, and escapists over the past four centuries.

PAGE 8
An early American checkerboard, in faded tones of simple black and white, hangs above a bed in the manner of a modern painting.

THIS PAGE
A gray barn door is decorated only by the simple curved outlines of its own handle and hinges.

PAGE 12
A slender door and wall, constructed of tongue-and-groove paneling known as wainscoting, are typical of American Country's utilitarian heritage. A simple, elegant backdrop for a minimal forged candlestick.

PAGES 14, 34, 86, 108, 128
Springtime in New England, an explosive celebration of the end of winter, when pink blossoms, green hedges, yellow field flowers, and purple skies make a dynamic theater for the senses.

For Danielle

© 1997 Herbert Ypma

First published in Great Britain in 1997 by Thames and Hudson Ltd, London

Published in 1997 and distributed in the U.S. by
Stewart, Tabori & Chang,
a division of U.S. Media Holdings, Inc.
575 Broadway, New York, NY 10012

Distributed in Canada by General Publishing Co. Ltd.,
30 Lesmill Road, Don Mills, Ontario, Canada M3B 2T6

Library of Congress Catalog Card Number: 96-72295
ISBN: 1-55670-556-5

Printed in Singapore
10 9 8 7 6 5 4 3 2 1

CONTENTS

INTRODUCTION

The "Country" of America has played a dominant role in shaping the nation's cultural expression.

Country was all the first settlers had. They arrived in a land with nothing more to offer than raw opportunity and raw nature. The Native North American, a true nomad, had left no building tradition: virgin forests, majestic mountains, and placid lakes were the pioneers' only resources. They quite literally built a nation from scratch, and it is their spirit of self sufficiency that remains at the core of American Country.

Today, the practicality and simplicity of the early settlers' approach to architecture and design continue to inspire, despite the fact that the greater part of the modern population have become city dwellers. Americans still aspire to the pure aesthetic of their origins. No wonder then that the art of the Amish and the craft of the Shakers speak more meaningfully to Americans than any cultural style imported from Europe. Together with shingle-clad saltbox houses and red clapboard barns, these legacies of America's pioneering days have assumed the status of cultural icons.

In New England, birthplace of the modern nation, the work of architects and designers continues to invoke the functional clarity of the first settlers. Red barns, weathered cedar shingles, and Shaker chairs are as old as America itself, but they remain a fountainhead of American style. Expressing the hardy, practical, and un-complicated spirit of the early settlers, American Country is a pure aesthetic, true to its Puritan roots.

1
ORIGINS

In architecture and design, American Country represents the ideals of purity and utility: reflections of the pioneering spirit of the people who dared to create a new nation from scratch.

AMERICAN

SALTBOX

"A plain wilderness, as God first made it" is how Captain John Smith described the America that greeted the first European colonists.

The pioneers left their old homes in the hope of making a better life for themselves in this New World. They came for many reasons: most came to practice their religion freely; others were farmers and tradesmen looking to improve their fortunes. Whatever the reason, within twenty years of the landing of the *Mayflower* in 1620, there were about two hundred thousand settlers in New England, and this wilderness was all they had, along with their liberty—and opportunity.

Despite their desire for change, the colonists brought traditions with them from England and Europe, including the manner in which they built their barns, fences, and houses. Doing what they had done back home was the quickest and most practical way to establish themselves in this new land. It also helped to assuage their yearnings for home. The look of familiar things provided a link with their roots.

Initially, the only discernible difference between Old and New World architecture was a sense of simplification. The skills needed for fancy detailing were often not available in colonial America and so the style of the settlers gradually became characterized by "doing without." With each successive generation, the local style became further removed from that of the mother country.

The so-called saltbox was the first uniquely American house to emerge. To Old World eyes, the forests of the New World seemed a boundless resource, and it was this abundance of wood that, architecturally speaking, shaped New England. Built in "post-and-beam" frame fashion, raised into place, and then sheathed in clapboard or shingle, the first settlers' houses started out as simple rectangular structures, usually containing four rooms grouped around a central chimney. The rooms were plain, with low ceilings, and small casement windows provided only dim lighting. Later, as demand for space grew, a lean-to would be added to the back of the house (usually housing the new kitchen and a storage attic), creating an asymmetrical gable roof, short on one side of the house and long on the other, and thereby changing the profile of the house to the one we now call saltbox.

Deriving its name from the shape of the small timber salt containers that were mounted on the wall of virtually every colonial kitchen, the saltbox house became the

architecture of choice for this frontier nation. In the beginning, it was a practical rather than an aesthetic decision. But this was an architectural style that would grow in popularity with the fortunes of the settlers. These homes reflected the colonists' roots in the Old World while at the same time demonstrating their adaptability and creativity.

The houses and furnishings that have survived from the time tell us a lot about the people who made or used them. Although 17th-century interiors, like the period's external architecture, were heavy and rectilinear, they were not entirely devoid of decorative painting or carving. Embellishment beyond utility, however, was used only sparingly, and was the hallmark of something of particular significance, as it would have involved many hours of lavish care and attention, a rare luxury in the survival economics of early colonial days.

Over time, these simple saltbox-shaped houses evolved into more balanced structures, reflecting the universal influence of classicism. Façades became more symmetrical and there was greater scope for interior decoration. However, utility remained the primary concern: characteristically, American colonials would look to European cities to see what was stylish and then simplify the forms. These new classics in timber spawned many offshoots and a new lexicon of descriptive terms had to be created: Greek Revival, Italianate, and Federal style. But America's architectural styles, diverse as they were, nonetheless had two key ingredients that together created a unifying indigenous signature: the ubiquitous use of timber, and the prevalence of symmetrical façades.

It is this legacy of simplicity and utility that makes American Country so pleasing to the modern eye. The spirit of the pioneers, the real and pure source of American style, is manifested in a building tradition which is still visible throughout New England. And nowhere is this style more in evidence than in the villages built by the Shakers.

PREVIOUS PAGE (16)

A great abundance of timber greeted the first settlers in the New World, and consequently almost all of the first structures, houses, and barns were timber-framed buildings, sheathed in strips of pit-sawed weatherboard (clapboard), mounted in an overlapping fashion.

PREVIOUS PAGES (18–19)

Named after the shape of the wall-mounted boxes used to store salt in almost all colonial kitchens, the saltbox home was the first truly American building. The Mulford House, which is depicted here, is one of the oldest surviving saltbox homes in New England.

OPPOSITE PAGE

Shingles split from American white cedar, a tree the settlers found in abundance in coastal swamps in the New World, provided a cost-effective, attractive, and what has become a distinctly American manner of cladding houses, barns, and public buildings.

SHAKER

SYMMETRY

If America is, as author Diana van Kolken writes, "a land of pioneers, dreamers, and idealists," then the Shakers should be considered not simply as a chapter in American history, but as fully the symbol of the spirit that shaped this new nation.

Founded by Mother Ann Lee in 1774, the Shakers (officially The United Society of Believers in Christ's Second Appearing, but rechristened "Shakers" by the public because of their "shaking" dance) shared a life of devotion to God, living in self-contained communities. As an expression of their devotion, the Shakers were dedicated perfectionists. In their pursuit of purity, they created beautiful objects that have survived the test of time.

It could be said that the Shakers were the first minimalists. The beauty of Shaker design derives from its perfect functionalism. Obsessed with order, cleanliness, and utility, they eschewed all forms of decoration and ornamentation. They had a saying that sums up their aesthetic quite succinctly: "Anything may, with strict propriety, be called perfect which perfectly answers the purpose for which it was designed."

The Shakers believed that they glorified God by striving to achieve perfection with their hands. The products of this pursuit of perfection—the furniture, tools, boxes, brushes, and bottles made by the Shakers—are today avidly sought out by museums, galleries, and private collectors.

Although, like the Amish, their doctrine stressed simplicity, plainness, and modesty, they were far from being "anti-technology." Indeed, they not only embraced advances from the outside world, but in their heyday, when membership exceeded six thousand in self-supporting communities from Maine to Kentucky, they were significant technical innovators themselves. In 1826, for example, they erected the famous round dairy barn at Hancock, Massachusetts, a design that permitted a single man, working in the center of the building, to feed and water all the cattle with a minimum of effort and motion. Among the many other inventions credited to the Shakers are the flat household broom, the circular saw, the clothespin, the double-chambered stove, the turbine waterwheel, and water-repellent fabric.

The Shakers were committed to balance and order, peace and harmony, in everything they did. This sense of "natural symmetry" governed their view of the world, even how they saw God. To the Shakers, God was both father and mother to mankind.

It was a dualism they were able to translate into the buildings in which they lived, prayed, and worked.

The Shakers sought, through symmetry, to establish absolute equality among the Brothers and Sisters. Each person had to be provided for, but in no manner better than the next. The Shakers were the first organized group in America to embrace women's rights and the notion of complete equality regardless of race or background, and it was this spirit of equality that dictated the design of their buildings.

Devoid of any decoration, the symmetrical architecture of the Shakers has endured both literally and figuratively, through the excellent quality of the craftsmanship and through the elegant simplicity of their aesthetic, which seems to have greater and greater appeal for modern sensibilities.

Particularly in the 1800s, when their numbers were at their peak, "Shaker" was synonymous with quality. They invested the best ingredients and craftsmanship available in their buildings. A list of materials used in the imposing brick dwelling-house built in 1830 in Hancock, Massachusetts, provides some insight into the Shaker commitment to doing things properly: 2,632 feet of white hewn stone, 565 feet of blue limestone, 350,000 bricks, 100 large doors, 245 cupboard doors, 369 drawers, 3,194 squares of glass in all… An impressive inventory by any standards, and made additionally impressive by the knowledge that each piece, each component, no matter how small or simple, was fitted or used with the greatest of craftsmanship.

Here, in the 1800s, was a group of people who practiced faithfully all the basic tenets of the 20th century's modern movement. "Form follows function" was a principle of the Shakers long before this century's leading architects made the phrase their guiding creed.

PREVIOUS PAGE (22)
The orderly, disciplined world of the Shakers was naturally predisposed to symmetry, as can be seen in the shape of the side of this meeting-house with a gambrel roof.

PREVIOUS PAGES (24–25)
This entrance to the dining hall of the boarding house at the Shaker village in Hancock, Massachusetts, is divided down the middle to accommodate the Brothers and Sisters equally.

PREVIOUS PAGES (26–27)
The meeting house of Hancock Shaker village was where the Shakers would assemble to pray, dance, and sing.

OPPOSITE PAGE
The short ladderback dining chair, here suspended from the ubiquitous Shaker peg rail (though historically it is unclear whether the Shakers hung their chairs), was designed to fit under the dining table to make clearing and cleaning easier.

FOLLOWING PAGES (30–31)
This portrait of three Shaker Sisters from the late 1800s is characteristically symmetrical, right down to the hair partings.

FOLLOWING PAGE (32)
Symmetry, discipline, and simplicity were applied to all things, including architecture.

FOLLOWING PAGE (33)
The louver atop this workshop roof illustrates early advances in sanitation techniques.

2

INTERIORS

The contemporary taste for refinement and simplicity has brought the basic styles of the early American settlers to the fore. A pared-down aesthetic, synonymous with chic, is the preferred direction for the modern interior.

AMERICAN

PORCH

"If New York City has an alter ego," write John Esten and Rose Gilbert in *Hampton Style*, "it is manifested here." New Yorkers flee for refuge to the Hamptons. On any given summer weekend, some of the world's most creative people can be found here.

The unassuming farmhouse owned by Alison Spear Gomez and her husband, Cuban-born Carlos Gomez, has always belonged to eminent members of the artistic community. *Vogue* editor and fashion legend Diana Vreeland used to come here to escape. Then it was George Plimpton, author and editor of the *Paris Review*, who would sit behind a desk in the attic study and write, looking out over the fields that once made this area the potato-producing center of colonial America. Now the house belongs to New York City-based architect Alison Spear Gomez and her husband, and from the porch of this "Shingle-style" structure, they continue the tradition of artists-in-residence.

It is a tradition that Alison Spear both respects and ignores. On the one hand, she has joined the many who flock to New York's favorite retreat, but on the other, she is not prepared to be swayed in the direction of whitewashed walls, Shaker furniture, and American folk art. Spear grew up in the Miami sunshine and she first started going to the Hamptons for the light, a quality that had attracted the American Impressionists one hundred years before. Light to her means color and that is what she has used as her principal decorative tool. Shades of vivid green, bright ocher, and deep earthy red have been used to define and accentuate the various rooms. At first glance, this rich, almost exotic approach would seem to be at odds with the whole notion of American Country, but in fact, bright colors were favored by those early settlers who could afford the luxury of richly colored paints. The 19th-century color card recreated on pages 104–105 shows how closely Spear's color scheme reflects the most popular pigments of the early days of the first American republic.

But there is more to Spear's signature than vibrant colors. Cuban modern art, flea market finds, oversize silver ornamental candlesticks, the occasional religious icon, and some 20th-century furniture classics demonstrate the eclectic taste for which she has become renowned in New York, where she is described as "the decorator for Manhattan's youngish F. Scott Fitzgerald set." This eclecticism, sense of space, and preference for vibrant colors can be traced to her unique background.

It was almost inevitable that Alison would become an architect. As a teenager, she was probably one of the last to witness life at the legendary Mar A Lago, the Florida retreat of Marjorie Merriweather Post. Together with her friend, who just happened to be the heiress's granddaughter, she would spend weekends in this architectural fantasy land. The chauffeur at the wheel of an old station wagon drove the two girls to the sugar-coated palace where they would be greeted by footmen in tails. Dinner was a scene straight out of a Fellini film: two little girls in a vast dining room attended by servants in fancy livery serving spaghetti from enormous silver platters, an experience that is reflected in Spear's design signature. There is a richness, a Baroque twist to her work that reflects the influence of the Rococo legacy of Mar A Lago.

Spear's only real concession to tradition lies in her approach to the exterior architecture. In addition to recladding the entire house in cedar shingles, she has also carefully removed or remodeled many of the cluttered and badly executed Victorian details to leave the house looking cleaner and simpler. The single most important improvement came from extending the original porch. The porch, that most American of architectural features, was originally limited to just the one façade. Spear's new porch wraps around the house's entire front exposure. From a practical point of view, it provides the space for outdoor entertaining. Furnished with white rattan, accented with the odd burst of color provided by cushions, candlesticks, and place-settings, it continues another great American tradition without pandering to it.

Alison Spear's interpretation of a plain farmhouse in the old potato fields of Sagaponack broadens the range of American Country. She has added another layer of possibilities without throwing away the ingredients that have made this style so uniquely American. From the porch of a part-colonial, part-Federal, part-Victorian, shingle-clad timber house, an American design tradition continues to evolve.

PREVIOUS PAGE (36)
The pristine new porch which wraps around the front and side of the house was architect Alison Spear's main alteration to this traditional "shingle-style" farmhouse.

PREVIOUS PAGES (38–39)
Symmetry, a keynote of houses built in the Federal style, is enhanced here by the carefully considered choice of decorative objects and furniture. Spear's use of bright color is unabashed. The painting, by Mendivé, is one of a substantial collection of works by young Cuban artists.

OPPOSITE
A deep red study corner provides the backdrop for a diptych by the photographer Ambra Polidori and a timber statue from a Cuban convent. Her furnishings and decoration purposefully avoid what Alison Spear calls the "Country clichés" of Shaker furniture, Windsor chairs, and Amish quilts.

FOLLOWING PAGES (42–43)
In what was originally the parlor, Spear has enhanced the boxlike space with a sunny ocher color and an eclectic selection of furniture. The windows, including the two flanking the fireplace, are original.

1	2	3	4	5	6
7	8	9	10	11	12
13	14	15	16	17	18

PHOTOS IN ORDER OF
APPEARANCE – PREVIOUS PAGES (44–45)

1

Unlikely objects, carefully chosen: shell balls on the mantelpiece typify Spear's approach to her interior.

2

"Carpenter Barbie," a suspended nude sculpted from a hammer handle.

3

A diptych by Ambra Polidori, an Italian photographer living in Mexico City, in a red corner of the main living area.

4

Exuberant color, gold and silver leaf, and objects antique and modern are the ingredients with which Spear has created her rich interior.

5

Another flea market find: a 1930s chandelier with a gold-leaf finish.

6

A painting by Argentinian artist Guillermo Kuitca stands in striking contrast to the dark red wall.

7

Four photos by Ambra Polidori displayed in an unusual corner setting.

8

The organic-shaped mirror frame, covered in raw silk, is one of Spear's own designs.

9

Clever use of color on the interior walls emphasizes the transition from one space to another.

10

A massive silver-leaf candlestick, typical of Cuban popular art.

11

The Federal origins of the building are clear in its recurring symmetry.

12 & 13

On sunny nights, the porch is the setting for dinner. The simplicity of the white-painted space is punctuated by a Cuban hurricane lamp decorated with a wild mosaic of glass tiles, and a bold composition of candy-colored dahlias.

14

The white-walled living room leads on one side to a yellow drawing room, on the other to a red alcove.

15 & 16

More examples of Carlos Gomez's extensive collection of contemporary Latin American art.

17

A colonial timber statue from a Cuban convent.

18

Climbing hydrangea against a timber wall of the poolhouse.

OPPOSITE PAGE

A pair of pineapple lamps in the poolhouse, complete with mini-pineapple screw threads, testify to Spear's daring, witty approach to decoration.

FOLLOWING PAGES (48–49)
The starkly simple, snowy white interior of the poolhouse sets it apart from the bright colors and rich textures of the main house.

FOLLOWING PAGES (50–51)
Furnishings in the poolhouse continue to reveal Spear's eclectic decorative sense: a pair of Bertoia chairs are combined with flea market finds.

COUNTRY

CONTEMPORARY

Today, city life is the everyday reality of most Americans. The label "American Country" really applies to the average lives of their 18th- and early-19th-century forebears. But while most people no longer live on farms, American Country remains deeply ingrained in the national psyche.

Every weekend, people flee the cities in droves and for a few days ensconce themselves in rural idylls. More than a century after America ceased to be a nation of farmers, the architecture, design, craft, food, and indeed rhythm of the "Country" continue to represent for many the American ideal. People long for shingle-clad cottages filled with folk art, Shaker furniture, and hand-crafted quilts. Old potato farms can command the type of prices that a château would sell for in Europe.

Why is this? Simply because Country, neither elitist nor bourgeois, is the popular American heritage. Take the Hamptons as an example. This historic corner of America has long been established as the favorite retreat of the blue-blazer, old-money elite of New York City. East Hampton, South Hampton, and Bridgehampton, the setting for *The Great Gatsby*, feature more than a handful of impressively grand weekend estates, and as early as 1875 an article in the *New York Times* described the area as "teeming with fancy blazers, innate with good breeding and family."

However, the first urban "escapists" to discover the Hamptons were actually artists eager to find an affordable place away from the city. In fact, two major art movements, American Impressionism in the late 19th century and Abstract Expressionism in the mid-20th, are inextricably entwined with the history of the Hamptons. Childe Hassam, Gaines Ruger Donoho, and George Bellows were the first to make the seasonal migration, starting in 1878, as part of a group called the Tile Club (an ironic reference to the contemporary preference for the decorative arts over "serious" painting). A second wave began in the Second World War: Fernand Léger, Max Ernst, André Breton, Marcel Duchamp, Willem de Kooning, Jim Dine, Larry Rivers, Roy Lichtenstein, Robert Gwathmey, James Rosenquist...It was here that Jackson Pollock bought a ramshackle farmhouse in 1945 and, influenced by Navajo sand paintings, did his first "drip paintings."

For the past century, then, artists have been vying for space with the local folk, and stories still abound about this "bohemian invasion" and the recurrent complaints

of East Hampton farmers "that they could hardly get past the artists and easels in their barns to milk the cows."

It may come as something of a surprise, but American Country is as much associated with the avant-garde art scene as it is with red barns, shingle style, and American quilts. The simplicity and purity of American Country are what first appealed to the creative eye, and the appeal continues to this day.

Without a doubt, the Hamptons have changed considerably since the first wave of escapists established this American tradition, but as John Esten and Rose Gilbert point out in their book *Hampton Style*, "whatever changes have come about have come with a certain gentleness. The past is always present."

The Hamptons have always managed to combine the rural with the modern and the conservative with the bohemian. This duality of spirit continues with the small shingle-clad cottage in the center of East Hampton that serves as winter and summer retreat for John Dean, partner in the very design-conscious Dean & Deluca chain of delicatessens, and Jack Ceglic, design director for Dean & Deluca.

Built in the 1920s as a worker's cottage and measuring only 20 x 27 feet, it could not by any stretch of the imagination be described as a rambling farmhouse. But the influences it draws on and the lifestyle its two occupants bring to it are in accord with the general love of nature and simplicity that American Country embodies. A unique quality of the house is how all the easily recognized ingredients of American Country—the Windsor chair, creamware jugs, simple furniture, a pot-bellied stove, wainscoting on the walls—have been utilized in a modern manner. It is a "transformation of tradition" that suits the spirit of the Hamptons very well indeed.

PREVIOUS PAGE (52)
The simple ingredients of a modern country retreat: a lambswool upholstered settee, cowhide rug, framed portrait, and sliding timber window.

PREVIOUS PAGES (54–55)
Symmetrically placed windows, a wood burning stove, a black-and-white tiled floor, a wing chair and couch covered with white cotton throws, and walls paneled in white wainscoting reflect the combination of simplicity and modernity in the Country aesthetic.

OPPOSITE PAGE
Creamware, the chunky, utilitarian pottery that has become synonymous with New World puritanism, is cleverly worked into the design scheme of this converted 1920s worker's cottage in East Hampton.

FOLLOWING PAGE (58)
This black-and-white Peacock chair by Danish designer Hans Wegner was inspired by the hooped form of the traditional Windsor chair which was very popular in America in the 18th century.

FOLLOWING PAGE (59)
A portrait of a horse, a chair designed by Dutch architect J. J. Oud, and the background of vertical lines form part of a rigorously geometrical still life.

FOLLOWING PAGES (60–61)
Situated at the back of the house, the sunroom overlooks the garden. It is divided from the kitchen by a small wall. The black-and-white color scheme and abundance of daylight contribute to the generous sense of space in this deceptively small interior.

FEDERAL

CLASSIC

"The taste which now reigns is that of the Antique. Everything we now use, is made in imitation of those models which have been lately discovered in Italy." So Archibald Alison described the new direction in American architecture in 1790.

The birth of a new nation is hardly a common occurrence and the first few years of the Federal Republic were heady times indeed. With all the talk of "the new Senate," it is no wonder the popular imagination was captivated by ancient Rome. Thus, in 1779, when George Washington took the oath of office and swore to uphold the recently ratified Federal Constitution, he ushered in a new era in American history, which brought with it a new style in architecture and furniture design, appropriately referred to as Federal style, the first phase of neo-classicism in America.

In England, the classical revival had been under way for some two centuries in one form or another, and by 1770 Robert Adam's neo-classical style was firmly established as the ideal. But the American settlers were delayed in their adoption of this new standard, being occupied with fighting the Indians and in any case more concerned with achieving independence from Britain than with imitating British styles. However, fired by the new-found political significance of the architecture of old Rome and driven on by a desire for increased luxury and comfort, by the end of the 18th century America was developing its own distinctive version of neo-classicism.

The type of home most Americans aspired to at the time is probably typified by the clapboard house now owned by Tom Woodard and Blanche Greenstein. It is a Federal classic, a piece of pure American heritage. Built by the founding family of the town of Fall River, Massachusetts (who, incidentally, came to America on the *Mayflower*), Ashley House is listed on the National Register of Historic Places because of its impeccable Federal detailing. It was once threatened with destruction by the local power company, and was saved only by disassembly, with each piece being labeled and carefully stored by Weatherhill Constructions, a company that specializes in this sort of work. The present owners bought the house (having seen it only in photos) and shipped it to an idyllic site in Wainscott, an old seaside farming community situated between the historic towns of East and West Hampton.

Two thousand individually numbered parts were transported to the new location and reassembled piece by piece. The beams, floors, staircase, and paneling doors are

original, and five thousand of the original bricks were used to recreate the five fireplaces, while the forty-one windows, all the hardware, and the interior shutters were reproduced from original documentation.

The most imposing original elements are the front entrance with its crown and elliptical fanlight, and the parlor with its impressive, formal symmetry and exquisitely detailed decoration, all executed in the simplified American version of neo-classicism that came to be known as the Federal style.

Yet despite this remarkable pedigree and the owners' scrupulousness in maintaining historical accuracy, the house does not suffer from being over-restored, nor does it feel like a museum. Instead, the interior feels throughout like a sophisticated interpretation of history; sparsely furnished with an overall palette that is, in fact, quite pale, it serves as an ideal setting for the owners' impressive collection of Country antiques, including folk art, painted farm furniture, quilts, and hooked rugs.

To explain the continuing appeal of the house, Tom Woodard quotes from Marcus Whiffen's *Eighteenth-Century Thesis of Williamsburg*, in which the three essential properties of architecture are identified as "commodity, firmness, and delight," qualities that his home has in abundance. The result, as Woodard describes it, is "a house for modern living, with the soul of an antique."

PREVIOUS PAGE (62)
In the Federal style, classical influences were married to New World ingenuity, as can be seen in the front door of this clapboard house. Lacking Old World masonry expertise, the builders fashioned the front steps from crude slabs of stone.

PREVIOUS PAGES (64–65)
Now set in a field near Long Island's fashionable Atlantic beaches, this house was originally built in 1780 for the Ashley family in Fall River, Massachusetts.

OPPOSITE PAGE
Decorated in a sophisticated palette of neutral shades and sparsely furnished with the owners' impressive collection of American antiques, the house

combines the advantages of a modern home with the patina, charm, and character of age.

FOLLOWING PAGES (68–69)
The influence of neo-classical symmetry and order is reflected throughout. A pair of tin pineapple urns flank a sundial above the fireplace, which is in turn flanked by a pair of reproduction Windsor chairs.

FOLLOWING PAGES (70–71)
In an upstairs bedroom, a piece of salvaged architecture in the form of a fan detail is framed by the shutters of the symmetrically placed windows.

FOLLOWING PAGE (73)
The upstairs master bedroom looks out over historic Wainscott Pond, an area untouched

by developers' bulldozers as a result of a neighborhood pact to preserve this scenic patch. A massive bay of windows and a decorative fanlight fill the room with light. The rugs on the floor are faithful reproductions of the original flat-woven rugs of the Shaker, Amish, and Pennsylvania Dutch weavers.

FOLLOWING PAGES (74–75)
Designer Tom Woodard readily admits he is not a purist. The interior is a combination of antiques, reproductions, and a modern sense of living. Particularly successful reproductions include the "fantail" Windsor chairs and the flat-weave colonial rugs, here juxtaposed with an old refectory table in the original parlor, now used as a dining room.

"I believe that buildings and mountains still

speak to us because they represent who we are

[and] where we are…but when I look to the left

and right of the highway, I become disturbed by

a perception that so much of our recent building

seems to litter, rather than to ennoble the world."

Kent Bloomer
Faculty of Architecture, Yale University
Turner Brooks: Work, 1995

DECONSTRUCTED

COTTAGE

The fountainhead of American architecture is its rugged colonial heritage. In other chapters, I have discussed the roots of American style: the clapboard saltboxes, the rough red barns, and the shingle-clad shacks and cottages that are attractive because of their imperfections and their rough unadorned structures. Yet, in the modern world, what is the equivalent of these American classics?

A few decades ago an interesting proposition was thrown into the architectural ring. The Californian Frank Gehry was one of the first architects to admit publicly to a problem that has plagued modern architects: most buildings look great when they are under construction but, as Gehry puts it, "look like hell when they're finished." He compared architecture to painting and found the former wanting: "There's an immediacy to painting, a sense that the brush strokes were only just made." That, in retrospect, is what the pioneers had going for them—no time to think or theorize, just the urgent need to build as quickly as possible, making the best of the materials at hand.

Unwittingly, or perhaps more accurately, unwillingly, Gehry started a movement to reintroduce these qualities of roughness and spontaneity to architecture, what he called the "expressive potential of raw structure." To the people who found his work ugly and unfinished, he would say: "To me, it seems we're in a culture made up of fast food and advertising and throw away and running for airplanes and catching cabs, etc.—in a word—frenetic. I think there's a possibility that these ideas about building are more expressive of our culture than to see something highly finished." Gehry was the father of deconstructivism. Using industrial and raw materials such as exposed plywood on the outside instead of concealed beneath plaster or paint, Gehry worked hard at creating buildings that look as if they just happened that way.

This approach to architecture appealed to East Coast architect Lee Skolnick, especially when it came to considering the design for an extension to a plain worker's cottage which had been built between the wars in historic Bridgehampton to house people working on the larger estates in the Hamptons. For years, the little house had been the summer retreat of design journalist and author Suzanne Slesin and her husband. The plain, single-story, rectangular box was perfectly suited to weekend escapes and the gentle rhythms of country life. But once children entered the equation, it was time to expand. One would not expect Slesin, a well-known author of high-profile style books, to take the safe approach in commissioning extensions to her cottage, and with the choice of Skolnick she didn't disappoint. Her decision, interestingly, brought together the charm and authenticity of "shingle style" with a new approach that not only calls on the power of raw structure and industrial ingredients, but also, like modern art, recognizes and plays to the restless nature of our gaze.

Rather than increase the volume of the cottage itself, Skolnick has chosen to add extensions linked by walkways and corridors. The original building is not only visible but remains the key visual element, with various new pavilions placed like building blocks on top of and beside it. The kitchen, on one side of the original cottage, mimics the traditional lean-to. The master bedroom is in a boxlike structure on stilts, from which the main living space can be viewed through a window in the *en suite* bathroom and can be reached physically by a bridgelike walkway constructed in exposed plywood. Indeed, all of the upstairs bedrooms are housed in separate structures.

However, this separation is only really apparent from the outside. From the inside, the spaces appear continuous, being linked, once again, by a series of walkways and corridors. Perhaps it was Gehry who originally drew the parallel between modern art and the modern eye, but for this project architect Lee Skolnick has taken the message to heart. The more one looks at the house, the more it reveals its spatial complexity. In true deconstructivist fashion, it appears at first glance to be free-form, the natural outcome of the combination of an indulgent client and a highly imaginative architect. The reality, however, is that Skolnick has created a three-dimensional puzzle that responds intimately to the demands of his clients. The resulting house is private, roomy, and visually playful, but still true to the original cottage at its heart.

Cedar shingles, wainscoting, plywood, copper pipes (as handrails), steel beams, glass, wallpaper: this house has all the ingredients found in the average American building... except that here, exposed plywood and shingles are on the inside.

The rustic, purpose-built charm of early modern America meets the unfinished poetry of deconstructivism. In all senses of the word, it is an American original.

PREVIOUS PAGE (76)

A simple worker's cottage was converted by architect Lee Skolnick into a family weekend home by the addition of structures executed in industrial materials such as plywood. These sit like sculpture on and against the outline of the original cottage.

OPPOSITE PAGE

In the main volume of the original cottage, the wall separating the kitchen from the living area provides an appropriate space for design author Suzanne Slesin to display her eclectic and eccentric collection of bowls, jugs, and flea market Americana.

FOLLOWING PAGES (80–81)

Architect Lee Skolnick relishes the continual play between outside and inside, not unlike Frank Gehry, to whom Skolnick attributes a debt of influence. The plywood walkway looks into the original space of the cottage and leads to the separate master-bedroom pavilion.

1, 4, 12 & 14

Her miniature chairs are a particular speciality among Suzanne Slesin's many collections. These are painted in the favorite bright shades of America's colonial past.

2 & 3

Bannisters made of copper piping are in keeping with the deconstructivist inversion of materials. Skylights ensure that all areas have light.

5 & 17

Viewed from the garden, the contemporary shapes of the new additions are softened by the majesty of the surrounding trees.

6 & 9

Barn red, as here, and colonial green are appropriate colors to accentuate the new Country architecture.

7

The master bathroom combines Skolnick's use of plywood with Slesin's idiosyncratic eye for interesting pieces.

8

Tea-stained chintz on a soft fluffy sofa contrasts with the more avant-garde architecture.

10

The copper box attached to the upstairs bedroom pavilion houses the fireplace, which is tucked into the corner of the master bedroom.

11

A flea market aficionado, Suzanne Slesin has filled the house with eclectic treasures.

13

An Adirondack chair in the garden has the patina of authenticity for which Suzanne Slesin has a keen eye.

15

Exposed beams and plywood panels reinforce the rugged simplicity of the original cottage.

16

A view from the single-story space of the original cottage reveals the unfolding complexity of the spaces created by Skolnick's extensions.

18

The shape of the original fireplace, now a free-standing island structure, echoes that of the staircase.

Opposite page

The living area near the free-standing fireplace is the transitional space between the traditional single-story volume of the cottage and the double-level space of the extension. The square cutout is a window to the upstairs master bedroom, while the door behind the floral couch leads to a spare room-cum-study.

3

COLORS

*The colors of American Country have always
been tempered by restraint and dictated by
practicality. From the soft, subtle blues and
yellows of the neo-classic Federal style to the
ubiquitous earthy red of the American barn,
these are the tones of a self-sufficient nation.*

BARN

RED

The red barn, a solid emblem of rural America. These austere, rather introspective buildings have a mythic, symbolic power, triggering strong feelings of nostalgia in even the most hardened of city-dwellers. "Proud silhouettes looming on the landscape," as Elric Endersby calls them, red barns are not just large sheds for shelter and harvest. They are wedded to that most ancient and civilized of activities, the tilling of the land, and they represent an enduring American tradition.

The barn was one of the basic utilitarian structures brought over by the early settlers from the Old World. But in America its form evolved and its status ultimately became iconic. Born of necessity and built with little regard for anything but practical use, the American barn was a direct embodiment of the survival instinct of the pioneers. One of the few resources readily available in colonial America was a plentiful supply of timber, which farmers were quick to exploit. Indeed, if it had not been for the abundant forests of the New World, the practice of timber construction might have died out altogether; by this date, timber framing in Europe was already doomed by the depletion of the forests.

The settlers rapidly adapted their structures to local conditions. Traditional features such as thatched roofs were abandoned, and in their place the pioneers adopted shingles split from the timber of the white cedar tree, which flourished in coastal bays and swamplands. A practical, durable choice, the same cedar was also used to make weatherboards for cladding the sides of barns. The overall size and shape of barns quickly evolved to accommodate changes in farming practices. Severe New England winters soon took their toll on unprotected livestock, and barns were expanded to provide seasonal shelter for animals and more storage space for hay.

Thus, the American barn developed into a distinctive structure, unique to America. In the words of John Fitcher, cultural historian at Sleepy Hollow historic village in New York: "New World barns are of noble proportions: the shape is neither squat and sunken nor narrow and tall. Even when viewed from a distance there is a quality of integrity about them: an integrity of purpose, of materials and craftsmanship, of complete adaptation to the conditions of their being."

Purely in design terms, the American barn had three essential, distinctive characteristics: the massive proportions and intricate complexity of its timber framing, the

distinctive shape of the gambrel roof, and the familiar red color.

All of these features expressed the pragmatic American spirit. The sheer size of many American barns made them particularly vulnerable to the forces of nature, especially wind, so to prevent the building from "going to rack and ruin" (an expression coined specifically for barns), timber framers used a complex of wind braces. Combined with the mass of the timber sections, these braces have a rhythmic sculptural beauty which is much imitated by modern American architects.

The gambrel roof was another distinctive innovation. The roofs of the earliest barns formed a triangular gable, but as farms grew in size and more hay was needed for greater numbers of livestock, ways to increase the loft capacity had to be found. One solution was to substitute a roof made up of two slopes on each side, the higher one more gentle, the lower steep.

Even the ubiquitous red was, once again, predicated on survival rather than aesthetics. Farmers protected their weatherboards with what lay to hand: a mixture of red oxides from their soil, linseed oil from their flax crop, and casein from the milk of their cows. This "homegrown" paint ranged in color from bright red to purplish brown, depending on the level of iron oxide present in the local clay. All these shades of red and brown are now known generically as "barn red."

It is not possible, from a colorist's point of view, to pinpoint an actual barn red shade, but this is ultimately not important. Local variations only add to our romantic fascination with barns. One thing is certain, however: no matter how imprecise the term may be, barn red has firmly entrenched itself as the most distinctive color of the American countryside. Set against the verdant green of an American summer or the pristine white of a snowbound American winter, barn red is an enduring visual icon of rural America.

PREVIOUS PAGE (88)
The most distinctive color of the American countryside is barn red. Vertically clad barns such as this example in Vermont appeared only after the introduction of sawmills to the New World. Earlier barns were either clad in clapboard (as on pages 2–3) or with shingles (as on page 107).

PREVIOUS PAGES (90–91)
The intensity of the red with which American barns were

painted depended on the level of iron oxide in the local clay: the more iron in the soil, the stronger the color.

PREVIOUS PAGES (92–93)
Massive sliding doors are a distinctive feature of American barns. They were introduced in the mid-1800s to prevent the doors banging shut or blowing open and possibly injuring livestock, as well as ruining the hinges that had to bear their substantial weight.

PREVIOUS PAGES (94–95)
There is no one specific shade of barn red: geographical variations range from brown to almost purple.

OPPOSITE PAGE
Early American settlers found the white cedar tree in abundance, and it proved a relatively easy timber to split into shingles. This gave rise to a distinctly American signature which is often referred to today as "shingle style."

AMERICAN

PAINT

Paint was a luxury in early America.

The story of American paint is the story of pigments. The presence of a particular color in colonial America was influenced by the price and availability of pigment. Paint as a ready-made product was a virtually unknown commodity. People would prepare their paint from dry pigments, linseed oil, natural varnishes, and other materials, according to their own personal recipes.

Procuring these ingredients, particularly in rural areas of 18th-century America, was no easy task: their availability was determined largely by ease of transport and the commitment of the entrepreneurial importer. White lead, red lead, vermilion, Prussian blue, Spanish brown, and yellow ocher were among the pigments that reached the colonial network. At the time the cities of Boston, New York, Philadelphia, Baltimore, Charleston, and Savannah were the centers of commerce and paint-making. Paint-makers, or "color men" as they were then called, sold pigments, varnishes, brushes, and other supplies. By the end of the 18th century, an established color man might have between twenty and fifty colors to offer.

Assembling the ingredients was, however, only the first stage of paint-making. The paint had then to be prepared. The main stage in this process was the laborious task of grinding. Since at least the 15th century, it had been known that the longer a pigment was ground with the binder (usually some type of drying oil), the better the color would be. A passage from Cennini's *Il Libro dell Arte* (1437) explains: "Take some clear water and grind this black for the space of half an hour, or an hour, or as long as you like; but know that if you were to work it up for a year it would be so much the blacker and better a color."

Basic grinding tools consisted of the Muller, a dome-shaped stone of varying size, and a slab, ideally made from marble. The color man moved the Muller in a circular motion by hand, forming a paste which was repeatedly pushed back under the Muller for further grinding. Because of the great amount of time and effort required to produce even the smallest amount of paint by this method, it is little wonder that paint was considered an especial luxury in early America. Even in the grandest houses, once a room was painted it would rarely, if ever, be repainted. These early paints, however, bear little resemblance to what we recognize today as paint. Rich in

99

PRUSSIAN BLUE (LIGHT)

MASSICOT

SPANISH BROWN

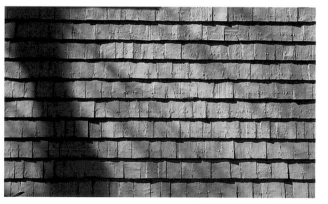

VERDIGRIS (LIGHT)

LIGHT WILLOW GREEN

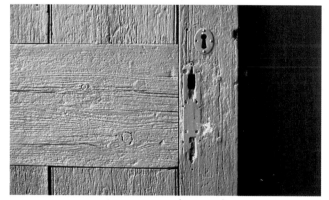

ASH GRAY

VENETIAN RED

OCHER

MINIUM

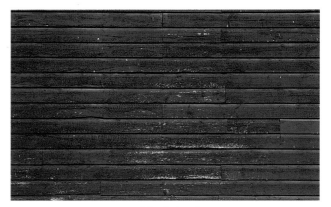

PRUSSIAN BLUE

LEAD COLOR

CLARET

CLARET (PALE)

WHITE

TERRE VERTE

STONE COLOR

pigment, they were more the consistency of paste than liquid, and it was therefore essential to rub them out in order to get a good coat. This was the skill of the painter or color man. Using large rounded bristle brushes known as pound brushes (because they could hold almost a pound of paste), early paints were worked onto the surface with great expertise in the direction of the grain of the timber. The reward was a finish with a depth, luster, and—most importantly—character that the thin and lifeless manufactured paints of today can in no way match.

So much handwork made a perfectly even finish impossible. But this only added to the aesthetic appeal of early American paint. It expressed the perfection of imperfection, an aspect of the decorative equation that has only recently started to gain acceptance once more.

PREVIOUS PAGE (98)

Spanish brown, one of the most famous historical pigments, and light verdigris, a pigment prized for its jewel-like green, are just two of the typical colors of American Country's heritage. The verdigris applied to this door of a historic farmer's cottage in upstate New York is typically oil-based, while the Spanish brown is a distemper paint, i.e., water-based.

PREVIOUS PAGES (100–101)

A massive clapboard barn and workshop in Massachusetts is a faded version of a color that would once have been described as claret: a mixture of Spanish brown and white. Since white pigment was often derived from white lead, the addition of white helped to preserve the paint's quality, protecting against termites and other wood-ingesting pests.

PREVIOUS PAGES (102–103)

These two individual doorways of clapboard-siding cottages demonstrate the subtle shadings of early American paints. Stone color, a combination of white with natural earth pigments, was mixed to resemble the color of fine limestone, and "terre verte," literally "green earth," was often mixed with white to produce a beautiful range of soft grayish-greens. Again, the addition of lead-based white was a practical, as well as an aesthetic decision.

PREVIOUS PAGES (104–105)

A typical early 19th-century American paint chart featured a selection of pigments which varied from simple iron-oxide- or clay-based browns and reds, to more exotic chemical colors from Germany, such as Prussian blue. The pigments were ground with a drying oil into a colored paste, which was then worked on to the surface in the direction of the grain of the timber, giving a finish with a far greater depth and texture than can be achieved with today's characterless paints.

OPPOSITE PAGE

*Spanish brown, a natural iron oxide pigment, is one of the least expensive readily available pigments. Historically, it was often used as a primer, but it was also used as a finish paint for kitchens and less important rooms. The **Builder's Dictionary** of 1731 recommends it not only for priming but also for finish painting of outbuildings and fences where aesthetics are not the primary concern. Many barns in New England are still painted this shade, which is included with all iron-oxide-based paints under the generic name "barn red."*

4

INGREDIENTS

The craft traditions of American Country mirror the pared-down practicality of colonial times. Amish quilts, Shaker chairs, and sturdy cream-colored china are still being made in a style that evolved out of the hard-scrabble existence of North America's early settlers.

AMERICAN

CREAMWARE

"Sanitary hotel china" is how painter-potter Henry Varnum Poor (1888–1971) sarcastically referred to the American ceramics tradition he so despised. From his perspective, the ubiquitous, thick, cream- or white-colored china had seemingly nothing more to offer than plain old function; it had little sense of art, refinement, or sophistication—ironically, the very hallmarks which give most American classics their appeal, particularly those born of Country origins.

The story of American creamware begins, as with almost all American domestic ingredients, with developments in Europe prior to the departure of the first wave of settlers to the New World. While the English and French were still busy producing earthenware jugs, German potters along the Rhine Valley had long since discovered that the local clay could be fired to an extremely high temperature to produce a material that was very dense—almost like stone—and which therefore offered significant advantages over earthenware pottery. However, this technique was kept a jealously guarded secret. It was not until 1671 that English potters finally discovered for themselves the method for producing this tough, salt-glazed "stoneware." (Salt-glazing involved introducing salt into the kiln, which combined with the silica in the clay to create a shiny, transparent coating.)

As early as 1730, potters initiated into the techniques of making fired stoneware arrived in America and set about finding local sources of clay to turn into practical containers. By the end of the 18th century, American stoneware had all but replaced earthenware as the domestic ceramics of this new nation. The English potteries continued to dominate the American market for decorative (as opposed to functional) ceramics, and fine bone china from factories such as Josiah Wedgwood's found its way to the tables of wealthy city-based colonists, as did the the treasured blue-and-white ware shipped in from China. However, American potteries were left to meet the domestic needs of simpler households, producing a wide array of strictly utilitarian vessels in stoneware. This was in the days before the introduction of canning or refrigeration, so housewives required a substantial number of containers for storing foodstuffs such as pickled vegetables, salted pork, vinegar, and homemade beer. Stoneware proved ideal for all these uses, not only because it was impervious to liquids and anything acidic (important in pickling), but also because, unlike older

earthenware glazes, its salt glaze contained no lead.

In the early days, production of stoneware was limited to New Jersey, Pennsylvania, and Virginia, because the clay came from these parts. As the market grew, however, and transport became more efficient and wider-reaching via the waterways and canals, New Jersey clay was shipped in increasing quantities to Vermont and upstate New York, where flourishing stoneware industries soon developed. The sheer volume produced by many of these simple workshops was often astonishing. One pottery, mentioned in a census carried out in 1850, had an annual output of one hundred thousand pieces of stoneware. Incredibly, this was achieved with a staff of just three men, one woman, and a horse!

By the end of the 19th century, with an upsurge in population and the increasing urbanization of life in the New World, small, family-run potteries had all but been obscured by large-scale factories. Only in isolated or mountainous areas did the tradition of the small pottery, producing utilitarian ware, survive into the 20th century. Nonetheless, the tradition did not quite die out. The preference for hardy, enduring pottery and china had established itself as a sort of fashion. Thus, American china continues to reflect the no-nonsense, utilitarian aesthetic which had originated in the days of the first settlers.

Exactly when the word "creamware" was first introduced into the American vocabulary is unclear, but from its very inception its application was as broad as the term "barn red." Creamware is a label that covers all "chunky" white- or off-white-colored crockery. Thick and sturdy, its proportions reflect the heritage of American stoneware. Today, it is highly improbable that you will go into a diner or café in America and not be served your food on solid, cream-colored crockery—yet the continual exposure of this "sanitary hotel china" in all walks of American life has certainly not dimmed its appeal.

PREVIOUS PAGE (110)

The popularity of the cream crockery of colonial America— chunky, practical, and of unaffected simplicity—has continued unabated into this century. It can truly be considered an early example of the modernist creed, "form follows function."

PREVIOUS PAGES (112–113)

Housed in a maple cupboard, this collection of creamware actually dates from the 19th century, but contemporary creamware still looks very much the same— the utilitarian simplicity of the 19th-century originals left little room for improvement.

OPPOSITE PAGE

The simple but robust style of American creamware gives it an enduring appeal. Its most copied and reinvented motif is probably the jug or pitcher, whose latest incarnation, by American designer Calvin Klein, can be seen on page 159.

FOLK

FURNITURE

"The peculiar grace of a Shaker chair is due to the fact that it was made by someone capable of believing that an angel might sit on it."

Thomas Merton's eloquent insight sums up the unique quality that has ensured the place of Shaker furniture as an acknowledged modern influence. Moreover, of all American furniture, only that of the Shakers can claim to be truly original. Unlike American Chippendale or the painted furniture traditions of Pennsylvania Dutch farmers, only the Shaker "style" was not in some way derived from an existing Old World style. It was, and is, an American original.

The purity and simplicity of Shaker theology were reflected in everything they did or made: their architecture, furniture, style of dress, even their food. In 1790, Joseph Meacham, the leader who succeeded the founder, Mother Ann Lee, set the tone for Shaker work when he enjoined the deacons to ensure that "all work done, be faithfully and well done, but without superfluity." This ideal was strictly adhered to. On one occasion, Brother David Bowley was directed to remove brass knobs and replace them with wooden ones, because they were "considered superfluous."

Though vanity was strongly condemned, craftsmanship of the highest order was encouraged. "Do all your work as though you had a thousand years to live on earth, and as you would if you knew you must die tomorrow," Mother Ann said. Excellent workmanship was a form of worship: Shakers believed that they glorified God by striving to achieve perfection with their hands.

In the late 1700s the Shakers began making chairs for sale. Indeed, as Diana van Kolken suggests, "the Shakers may very well have been the first chair manufacturers in this country." By 1852, the Shakers from the New Lebanon community in New York were making and selling their chairs in large quantities. They issued catalogues and, in a manner typical of their orderliness, divided the chairs into a range of sizes from zero to seven, with fourteen different woven cotton-tape options for the seats.

"Shaker-made" became synonymous with "well-made," a reputation that no doubt helped in turning the production of chairs into a major business. The 1869 catalogue of Robert M. Wagan's Shaker chair factory at Mount Lebanon declared: "We have spared no expense or labor in our endeavors to produce an article that cannot be surpassed in any respect, and which combines all the advantages of durability,

simplicity, and lightness." Many agreed. Wagan's factory turned out six hundred chairs in the first nine months of 1869 and the business, despite the founder's death in 1883, continued uninterrupted until 1942.

For the majority at the time, however, the simplicity of the Shaker aesthetic made too violent a contrast with the prevailing taste. Charles Dickens's impressions of the community at New Lebanon are representative: "We walked into a grim room, where several grim hats were hanging on grim pegs, and the time was grimly told by a grim clock, which uttered every tick with a kind of struggle, as if it broke the grim silence reluctantly, and under protest. Ranged against the wall were six or eight stiff, high backed chairs, and they partook so strongly of the general grimness, that one would much rather have sat on the floor."

Today, in a world where pared-down has become synonymous with chic, Shaker is fashionably stylish. Although the authentic Shaker furniture-makers are long gone, fine craftsmen still use their methods and designs. Numerous firms in America devote all their energies to the manufacture of faithful Shaker reproductions, several antique dealers concentrate almost exclusively on Shaker Americana, and auctions dedicated to Shaker items are widely advertised and heavily attended. There are specialized Shaker boutiques in some of the world's most cosmopolitan capitals, including London and New York, and a French woman, Elisabeth Jaeger, living in the Lot region, has carefully studied their techniques and now creates Shaker copies for sale in France that are fully worthy of this great tradition.

Ironically, as the reputation of their design continues to grow, the Shakers are in danger of dying out: there remain only a handful of members in the last surviving Shaker community of Sabbath Day Lake in Maine. Nonetheless, their influence in design seems secure.

PREVIOUS PAGE (116)

Shaker furniture has taken its place among the most highly prized and collectable examples of early American craftsmanship. The appeal of its combination of elegant proportions and reassuring restraint, exemplified in this maple bureau and ladderback chair, has, if anything, increased, and many designers and architects have paid homage to the pared-down aesthetic of the Shakers in their own work.

PREVIOUS PAGES (118–119)

In addition to furniture, the Shakers also devoted considerable time and effort to the making of practical items such as boxes and brooms. In fact, the Shakers are often credited with having invented the modern broom. Although they were hardly the first to think of bundling straw together to make a cleaning tool, they did invent a machine that could make brooms on an industrial scale. Thus, in 1860, three broom

manufacturers based in Hancock, Massachusetts, could lay claim to the production of 16,500 brooms, which were worth a total of $2,934.

OPPOSITE PAGE

Perhaps the most famous and enduring example of Shaker furniture is the ladderback rocking chair with a woven seat. Even President Kennedy owned one. It was the chair to which he would retire when he was suffering from a bad back.

AMISH

QUILTS

"A splash of color in the quiet of the land" is how one observer has described the extraordinary quilts of the Amish.

Perhaps the most remarkable thing about these quilts is the very fact that they were made by the Amish. Their artistry is undeniably exquisite, yet art for the sake of art was frowned upon in the Amish communities. What is all this color doing in a world of black hats, drab carriages, and stern faces?

The simplest explanation would be to put it down to a Shaker-like notion of form following function. Certainly, the Amish, like the Shakers, have a longstanding tradition of craftsmanship, performing the most mundane tasks with pride and care; but Amish quilts are more finely made than function alone could justify. The extravagant stitching far exceeds what is necessary to keep a quilt intact. Amish quilts are sheer celebrations of the beauty of quilting.

Quilting was no more an American invention than the all-American barn. It was a craft brought over from the Old World by the settlers. Quilts were an essential, practical ingredient of colonial life. Pioneers heading west wrapped their valuables in them, used them as cushions on their hard wooden seats, and padded the canvas walls of their wagons with them as a protection against Indian attack. Quilts were, quite literally, present from the cradle to the grave: new-born babies were wrapped in them, and in the Midwest, where there was little timber for wooden caskets, quilts were used as burial cloths.

They even became political tools. Once the Civil War had broken out in 1861, soldiers would set out on the battle trail with a homemade quilt for warmth and comfort, while American women came to rely on their quilt-making abilities as a means of raising money for everything from firearms to bandages. More than twenty thousand soldiers' aid societies were formed across the country and quilt auctions were the source of much of the money raised.

The making of quilts was therefore already an American institution before the Amish took up the craft. In the words of Roderick Kiracofe in *The American Quilt*, "For more than a hundred years American women had been recording their hopes and dreams, their fears and frustrations, in the exciting stitches and exuberant designs of their quilts."

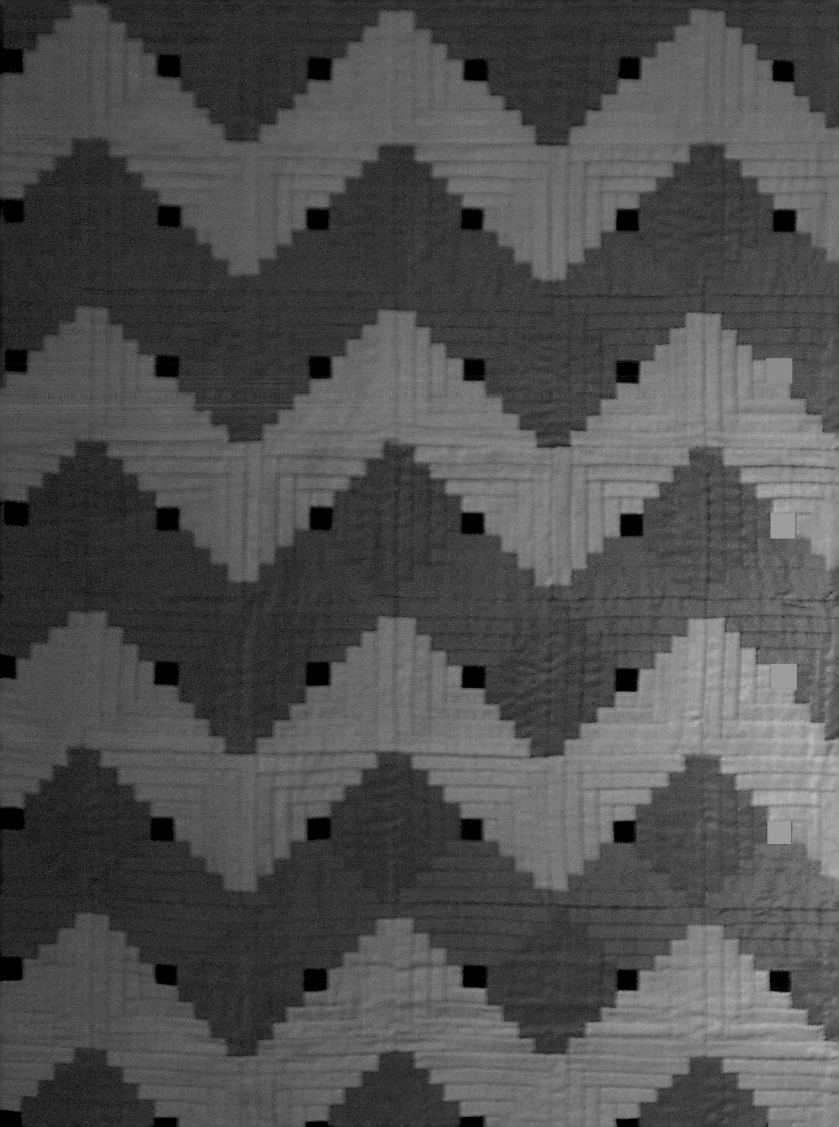

The Amish had no tradition of quilting in their original culture. Amish women learned the skills from their non-Amish neighbors in Pennsylvania in the mid-1850s, and in the space of a single generation became expert quilters. Such are the historical facts. However, they hardly explain the extraordinary creativity and colorful vibrancy of Amish designs. For that we must look to Amish culture.

Contrary to popular belief, the Amish do not in fact spend their entire lives dressed in somber tones of black. Children dress in vibrant blues, greens, purples, pinks, and dark reds, and adults often wear vivid colors beneath their black overcoats or use colorful fabrics to line their black garments. Quilts are often made with the scraps of material left over from these colorful clothes. Their true power, however, lies in the manner in which the colors are combined. In *The World of Amish Quilts*, Rachel and Kenneth Pellman suggest that the Amish sense of color is a direct result of the community's self-imposed isolation. The Amish approach is unworldly, naïve, and unconcerned with fashion; their creative instincts are untutored compared with those of the "modern" person living in a city. But it is this very lack of formal aesthetic education that permits a more daring freedom and explains the occasional bursts of vibrancy alongside the subtle blends of shading.

The same applies to the inspiration of their designs. Like Islam, the Amish faith forbids figurative representations of God's creations; thus the quilters fall back on pure geometrics for inspiration. The patterns reflect in an abstract sense everyday aspects of their lives, from stacked blocks of hay in the field, long stretches of plowed furrows, and horizontal slats on wooden fences, to the round wheels of buggies and the stars in the sky.

But the Amish bring a further, vital ingredient to their work: tension. These quilts are the colorful expression of a people for whom individual expression is normally discouraged. Limited in their access to color in their everyday lives, in their quilts the Amish create an almost uninhibited world of color … "a splash of color in the quiet of the land."

PREVIOUS PAGE (122)

One of the oldest and simplest quilt patterns is the Center Diamond, or Diamond in Square. Here, the center square features the Sunshine and Shadow pattern widely used by the Amish of Lancaster County, named after the light and dark effect created by combining a variety of bold, solid colors.

PREVIOUS PAGES (124–125)

A favorite among quilt makers, the Log Cabin pattern thrived in Amish and Mennonite communities. Made of long, narrow pieces of fabric, or "logs," which were "stacked" on top of each other, the pattern evokes the geometry of a barn under construction or the simple lines of stone church steps.

OPPOSITE PAGE

Tumbling Blocks is a simple quilt pattern which through interplay of color and apparent dimension creates the illusion of stacked cubes. Inspired by the blocks of straw stacked in barns for the long American winter, the three-dimensional effect relies on the use of three fabrics in varying intensities of color.

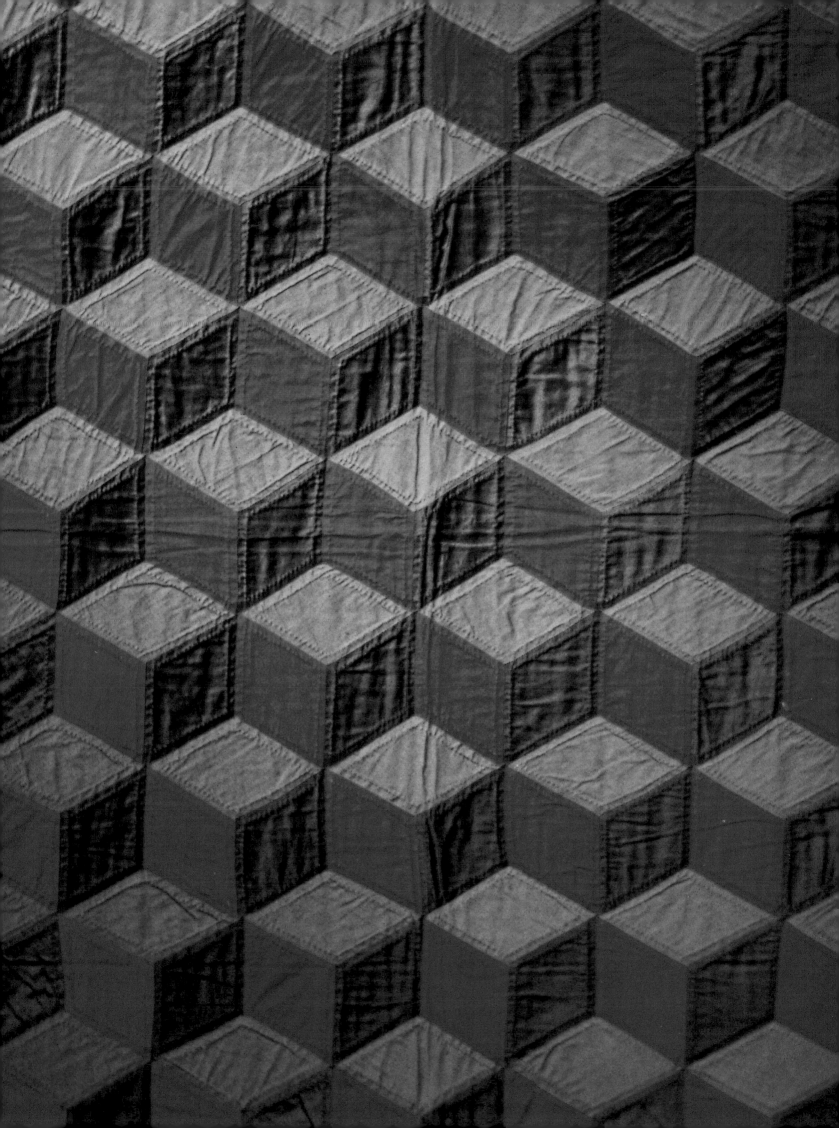

5

VIRTUOSI

American Country is more than a nostalgia for the purity of the past. The shapes and materials of colonial times often provide the starting point for new design and architecture.

TURNER

BROOKS

Turner Brooks has a different perspective on American Country from most: he actually lives in the heart of dairy country in deep Vermont and commutes into the city. His trip to work takes him along scenic Route 9, a narrow country road that winds and meanders its way past real farms and rural communities and eventually leads to the turnpikes and superhighways that mark the end of country innocence and tranquility. It is a journey that has helped shape his view of how he prefers to build.

Brooks's favorite book as a child was Virginia Lee Burton's *The Little House,* which tells the story of a farmhouse that sits atop a picturesque knoll in an idyllic pastoral landscape. One day a road is laid across the hill, directly in front of the house, and the peaceful rhythm of rural life is destroyed as skyscrapers eventually rise up above the house and a subway is dug beneath it. Finally, the farmer and his family decide to abandon their home. All seems lost for the little farmhouse until a relative of the farmer comes to the rescue. The house is placed on the back of a truck and for a brief moment all the frantic activity of the city halts in a kind of salute as the farmhouse sets off in triumph back to the country.

Brooks's affection for this story not only says much about his feelings for the country, but also about what he sees as the right relationship between the land and the buildings on it. As he says, "When I first moved to Vermont I found myself drawn to some of the more shack-like and scruffy buildings scattered *en route.*" Mobile homes, clapboard cottages, and lean-tos seemed to him as if they were "motoring across the landscape under their own power, alone, as a ship is alone on the sea," an appearance which struck him as appropriate for buildings whose inhabitants have a far less stable relationship with the land than their forebears. This is an architecture in an honest relationship with a landscape "where the old agricultural order is disintegrating rapidly."

As farms deteriorate, fields turn to bush, and the mighty forests of New England start to encroach again on the once neatly defined agricultural spaces of traditional farms. These tiny houses, which "touch the earth lightly," do not need an extended, man-made agricultural landscape to anchor them. Instead, Turner Brooks sees his buildings as compact bodies that are placed on the land without "any presumption or ambition of transforming it."

131

This "notion of motion" has always had an important place in his thinking. Brooks even relates the interiors of his houses to the idea of driving across the landscape. For this reason his houses are deeply American. As Jonathan Schell notes in his critique of Brooks's work, "there is more motion than stability in the history of the American landscape." This landscape is being continually obliterated and rebuilt in what economist Joseph Schumpeter called the "creative destruction" of the free market—the same cycle of destruction and rebuilding that is at the heart of *The Little House*.

Brooks's notion of buildings moving through the landscape may be seen to be part of a larger, ecologically progressive movement. Half a world away, in Australia, architect Glenn Murcutt is also concerned with "touching the earth lightly," the idea of buildings not affecting or influencing the land on which they sit. In an environmentally aware world this seems an entirely proper direction for architects to be taking.

And there are also practical considerations. "Touching the earth lightly" means not having to dig and pour expensive foundations. And "floating free on the landscape" means no expensive and tedious landscaping, leveling, or gardening. The result is affordable and appropriate housing.

Brooks may have a different take on American Country, but the houses he builds are nonetheless familiar and reassuring. He loves the materials in which the simple little houses of rural America are clothed. He has a real affinity for clapboard siding, weathered shingles, and the red of traditional American farm barns. As Kent Bloomer, professor of architecture at Yale, points out about his former student: "His houses seem to possess a regional classicism, as though they had been there for a long time." The windows, doors, clapboard, trim, and posts are characteristic of Vermont. It's just the way he uses these elements that is different. There is nothing nostalgic about Brooks's houses, nothing of what Jonathan Schell calls "groping for American roots." Bloomer continues: "To analyze all of Turner Brooks's houses is to find the same elements of economy, classicality, sculptural resolution, and pervasion of the landscape that epitomize the Peek House."

In fitting conclusion, Bloomer notes: "I become disturbed by a perception that so much of our recent building seems to litter rather than to ennoble the world. But his [Brooks's] buildings calm me down. His sensitive figures in the landscape have humility. They buttress my faith in the act and grandeur of architecture."

PREVIOUS PAGE (130)
Turner Brooks believes even small buildings can make grand gestures. The sculptural form of his Peek House stands proud and elegant against the skyline.

PREVIOUS PAGES (132–133)
The Peek House is in perfect harmony with the Vermont landscape, whose fields, rivers, mountains, and lakes are all integral to Brooks's work.

OPPOSITE PAGE
Brooks combines a distinct approach to architecture with a preference for traditional materials, such as clapboard siding and barn-red-colored paint.

DEAMER
PHILLIPS

Three pebbles and a book... that's what the clients brought to the first meeting with husband-and-wife architectural team Deamer Phillips to discuss plans for a weekend retreat.

The pebbles were collected from nearby Gibson Beach in Sagaponack. Sea-washed and sun-bleached, in tones of off-white and light gray, they evoked the light, open, and natural mood the clients were looking for. The book was about Shaker furniture and objects. Architects Peggy Deamer and Scott Phillips were already Shaker enthusiasts, so from the beginning there was a shared sense of purpose.

"Stark and modern, yet very soft" was the clients' brief. Deamer Phillips responded with a design scheme reminiscent of the noblest of American Country influences. From the basic building materials to the orientation of the house, Shaker notions of symmetry, purity, practicality, and simplicity were applied.

The house stands on eighteen acres of land, bounded on one side by potato fields and on the other by a nature reserve dense with indigenous trees: an appropriate setting for a truly American building. In deference to the unspoiled character of the site, and to accommodate their clients' request for privacy combined with the capacity to house guests, the basic structure of the building began to emerge more as a group of separate structures than as one large, overbearing building. The serene aesthetics of a Shaker village provided the model. The project evolved as a small gathering of traditionally shaped, gable-roofed, shingle-clad pavilions connected by elegant, light-filled corridors. As in Shaker villages, a great deal of attention was paid to the grouping of the various buildings.

The structures were ranged around the sides of a central "lawn" (which resembles a village green), and in the manner of Shaker villages each "house" was assigned a separate and distinct function. The largest building, the Long Room, a rectangular, hall-like space, is eerily reminiscent of a Shaker meeting hall and, fittingly, it was intended for the family's communal activities, such as eating, drinking, and just plain lounging about.

Another group of buildings house the children's bedrooms and yet another, facing the Long Room across the lawn, was earmarked for use as the master bedroom. On the other side, connected by a glass-lined, light-filled, slender corridor, is the only

two-story building in the complex. It was designed to be a completely self-contained, private retreat for guests. Further afield, buildings with less domestic functions, such as the garage, the tennis court pavilion, and the poolhouse, complete the architectural language of the house-as-village.

In keeping with rural American tradition, all the buildings were clad with cedar shingles. Fieldstone was chosen for the foundations of the various structures, as well as for the retaining wall dividing the "lawn" from the fields surrounding the house. Again, this is a manner of construction that can be traced back to the very beginnings of New World architecture, as a comparison with the barn foundations illustrated in photo 3, page 95, shows.

Following Shaker tradition, the overall construction was carried out according to a policy that can be described as "simple but solid." There was certainly no skimping on materials. Window and door frames were fashioned from solid mahogany, and beautiful blond timbers like beech were used for all the built-in closets and cupboards. In fact, as Phillips readily owns, the design "started with the cupboards."

PREVIOUS PAGE (136)
Taking its inspiration from the simple beauty of Shaker craft and design, this Sagaponack, Long Island home features beautiful built-in beech shelving throughout.

PREVIOUS PAGES (138–139)
In imitation of a Shaker village, the house was conceived as a series of separate structures. The view of the verdant lawn from an adjoining field beyond the perimeter wall demonstrates the village-like intent of the design.

PREVIOUS PAGES (140–141)
The main entertaining space is in a long rectangular building that resembles the Shaker dining room illustrated on pages 24–25. Attention to detail is the highlight of this house, and perhaps only the people who worked on it, from the land-

scaping team to the carpenters, can really appreciate how much work it takes to achieve simplicity.

OPPOSITE PAGE
Connecting the Long Room with the buildings housing the bedrooms, this corridor provides a clear sense of transition from one kind of space to the next. Sunny and window-lined, all the fine detailing, including the wall lights, was designed by the architects. Everywhere you look, there is symmetry, order, and balance. The arrangement of the built-in storage units on the left-hand side was designed to provide a patterned counterpoint to the wall of glass doors on the right.

FOLLOWING PAGES (144–145)
This view from the pond reveals how the architectural composition resembles the traditional

positioning of outhouses and shacks of colonial villages. Details such as shape, window size, and the choice of cedar shingles demonstrate a consistent commitment to historical continuity.

FOLLOWING PAGES (146–147)
In the Long Room, interior designers Carlson Chase worked from a discreet palette of neutral naturals to achieve the casual, sun-bleached atmosphere that the owners had in mind. Within the highly refined shell created by architects Deamer Phillips, they introduced sofas of their own design in the pale, refined textures of natural cottons, rugs designed in conjunction with V'Soske of New York, the delicate patina of Flischi table lamps, and the blond simplicity of the custom-made aspirin-shaped occasional tables.

1	2	3	4
5	6	7	8
9	10	11	12
13	14	15	16

PHOTOS IN ORDER OF
APPEARANCE – PREVIOUS PAGES (148–149)

1

The bedrooms are distinguished by the warmth of the beech-faced, built-in storage.

2

The smallest details have been considered. A spice rack is incorporated into the galvanized frame of the kitchen.

3

The master bedroom, in a different building, features even more elaborate built-in furniture. It is separated from the Long Room by an expanse of lawn and connected by the corridor depicted on page 143.

4

Strategically placed throughout the house, beech-framed "cutouts" house the owners' collection of artisan pottery.

5

The breakfast corner, featuring a table designed by Carlson Chase, is a pivotal space connecting the corridor with the Long Room.

6

A corner of a guest bedroom is distinguished by a still life of modern design classics, including a Post chair by Viennese turn-of-the-century architect Josef Hoffmann and a custom-designed webbed chair that is a more generous interpretation of its Scandinavian original.

7

A significant feature of the design is the daylight that streams in through the elegant doors which extend the length of one wall of the Long Room.

8

Work surfaces in the kitchen, designed as a free-standing island at one end of the Long Room, are illuminated by custom-designed galvanized spotlights.

9

Black-and-white photos from the owners' collection, framed in simple timber moldings, are the only addition to the otherwise pristine walls.

10

The living area, arranged around the second of two fireplaces in the Long Room, is a soft, subtle, but sophisticated combination of lamps by Flischi, custom-designed occasional tables, and a single framed photo on the cantilevered stone slab mantelpiece.

11

Natural textures and natural fibers, employed in a casual organic fashion, provide the theme of the interior.

12

The Long Room benefits from two fireplaces placed at the two main meeting points, one at the end of the dining table and the other at the end of the living area.

13

An extended view of the Long Room demonstrates the generous volume of this light-filled space. The suspended ceiling lamp was designed by Carlson Chase.

14

The beech built-in storage is distinguished by beautiful detailing, such as the triangular timber door pulls.

15

The kitchen combines stone work surfaces and galvanized steel to create a solid impression of utilitarian simplicity.

16

A diagonal wall creates an intimate, light-filled space at the other end of the Long Room. The faux-zebra-patterned armchair, designed by Alvar Aalto, adds to a formidable collection of pedigree furniture.

O
OPPOSITE PAGE

Influenced by Shaker architecture, Deamer Phillips placed tremendous emphasis on symmetry, simplicity, and a high standard of craftsmanship.

The owners' request for storage space for blankets and quilts provided the architects with another opportunity to pay homage to the Shakers. Designed to be out of the way and invisible, the recessed cupboards began as a utilitarian detail, but have actually turned out be one of the most beguiling features of the house. "Closets were part of the architecture," says Phillips. The positioning of the built-ins has resulted in a pleasing, rhythmic design, "a pattern as a result of the placement of functional elements, not pattern for pattern's sake," as the architects are quick to point out.

Contrary to popular belief, the Shakers, concerned with quality and craftsmanship in all their endeavors, were not cheap or conservative when it came their commitment to achieve the best possible results. The famous round barn in Hancock, Massachusetts, for example, was constructed with the help of fifty-three highly skilled masons, at a cost of $15,000—which at the time was an absolutely extraordinary sum to spend on a barn.

It is a lesson that the architects and clients took to heart. The finest carpenters and cabinet makers were given the freedom to work in a way that ensured the best possible results, as were the team of landscapers that designed and installed the seemingly effortless and completely natural garden, and the masons who laid the fieldstone foundations.

In fact, from the point of view of quality, it is difficult to imagine how one could improve on what has been achieved. Stacked fieldstone foundations and shingle cladding echo the strongest details of early New World utilitarian buildings, and the arrangement of the collective structures evokes the serene beauty of the Shaker village. Inside, there is superb craftsmanship based on the solidest principles of utility and practicality. The entire house has been constructed with a rigorous refinement and precision that is normally found only on yachts. Yet the design gives the impression of simplicity and restraint. The humble origins of early American design and architecture have been mirrored in the most flattering, practical, and modern manner. The barns and villages of rural America are reflected in a building which recreates, without corny nostalgia, the true essence of American Country.

PREVIOUS PAGE (152–153)
The vast proportions of the Long Room are demonstrated by the fact that it can so easily accommodate a table to seat twelve. The refectory-style solid maple table was designed by Carlson Chase and inspired by Shaker furniture. The chairs were originally designed by Paul Matthieu and Michael Ray for the Ford modeling agency in Paris. The massive scale is beautifully balanced by the refinement of the detailing, exemplified in the construction of the support beams to the right of the photo.

OPPOSITE PAGE
The illuminated connecting corridors not only provide ideal display space for the owners' collection of artisan pottery; they also play an important role in the overall success of Deamer Phillips's design for this Sagaponack retreat.

ACKNOWLEDGMENTS

No book, and particularly no illustrated book, ever becomes a reality without the help of a lot of people. In particular, I would like to thank Alison Spear Gomez and Carlos Gomez, Suzanne Slesin, Jack Ceglic and John Dean, Tom Woodard and Blanche Greenstein, Peggy Deamer and Scott Phillips, Don Carpentier, Peter Carlson, and Turner Brooks. Without them, this project would never have been completed. Thank you.

BIBLIOGRAPHY

Emmerling, Mary. *American Country Classics*. New York: Clarkson Potter, 1990.

Endersby, Elric, Alexander Greenwood, and David Larkin. *Barn*. London: Cassell, 1992.

Esten, John, and Rose B. Gilbert. *Hampton Style*. Boston: Little, Brown & Company, 1993.

Fitzgerald, P. Oscar. *Four Centuries of American Furniture*. Radnor, Pennsylvania: Wallace Homestead, 1995.

Harlow Ott, John. *Hancock Shaker Village*. Hancock, Massachusetts: Shaker Community, Inc, 1976.

Johnson, James, David Larkin, and June Sprigg. *Colonial*. New York: Stewart, Tabori & Chang, 1988.

Kiracofe, Roderick. *The American Quilt*. New York: Clarkson Potter, 1993.

Murray, Stuart. *The Shaker Heritage Guidebook*. Spencertown, New York: Golden Hill Press, 1994.

Pellman, Rachel and Kenneth. *The World of Amish Quilts*. Philadelphia: Good Books, 1984.

Slesin, Suzanne, Stafford Cliff, and Daniel Rozensztroch. *New York Style*. New York: Clarkson Potter, 1992. London: Thames and Hudson, 1992.

Turner Brooks: Work. New York: Princeton Architectural Press, 1995.

Van Kolken, Diana. *Introducing the Shakers*. Bowling Green, Ohio: Gabriel's Horn Publishing, 1985.

SHAKER

BOXES

"If you can put it down, you can put it away." This was the creed by which the Shakers lived. *"You will never get into heaven unless you're clean,"* Mother Ann would admonish the Brothers and Sisters, and as a result, storage became an important theme in their craft. The boxes of Brother Delmer C. Wilson (1873–1961), of the Sabbath Day Lake community in Maine, were celebrated worldwide. Shaker Workshops of Massachusetts believe their boxes, handmade in cherry timber, measure up to these high standards. The Shakers used them for sewing bits and dry kitchen goods, but they can be adapted to suit most needs.

Tel. 1-508-827-9900
1-800-840-9121

HISTORIC

PAINT

Paint today is a shadow of its former self. It used to be a thick, pigment-packed, pastelike substance that would add depth and luster to a building. Now we have thin, easy-to-apply liquids that virtually guarantee an even finish. But who wants an even finish? It stands to reason that the current interest in the characterful imperfection of old buildings should create a demand for paints that are equally rich in character and integrity. A New England firm called Historic Paints now makes a range of paints with the dynamic and texture of the 18th- and 19th-century originals.

Tel. 1-607-293-8184
1-800-664-6293

SHAKER

FURNITURE

Often ridiculed in their day, the simple style of the Shakers is now very much in demand. Since original items are priced outside the range of most pockets, reproduction pieces are now the best bet. One company in particular has dealt cleverly with the question of "finished" quality by offering faithfully reproduced Shaker furniture in self-assembly kits. It is also, in spirit, far closer to the Shaker original ideal, in that the furniture is provided at a reduced cost and gives one an opportunity to use one's hands. Shaker Workshops of Massachusetts provides a "Shaker's guarantee" on all their work.

Tel. 1-617-648-8809
1-800-840-9121

ADIRONDACK

CHAIR

The Adirondacks are now legendary because of their unique design tradition. Twigs, roots, burl, silver birch, and cedar were transformed into furniture and decoration, creating a magical setting which almost blurred the distinction between interior and exterior. Perhaps the slatted wooden armchair got the name "Adirondack chair" as a general acknowledgment of the influence of Adirondack craftsmen. Whatever its exact origin, the Adirondack chair has become an American favorite. This one is appropriately a cleaner, more modern interpretation of the handmade originals.

Tel. 1-415-540-7154

WINDSOR

CHAIR

...erson had black and gold ones, and ...Franklin ordered them in white, but ...common color was green. Originally ...d from England, the Windsor chair ...y became an American favorite. Made from ...al different woods and therefore always ...nted, their strength and economy made them ...perfect for rugged New World use. Perhaps because of the Windsor chair's association with the greatest of America's founding fathers, it has become a very patriotic piece of furniture. This "fantail" Windsor is a faithful reproduction made in New England.

Tel. 1-212-988-2906
1-800-332-7847

CONTEMPORARY

CREAMWARE

Creamware is another example of how the early American penchant for utility and simplicity pervades contemporary everyday American life. The pioneers needed plates and cups that could survive bone-rattling journeys in covered wagons. Creamware, a tougher, thicker version of bone china, was the answer. Today, commercial establishments still exploit its robust nature, but the simple style of creamware has also undergone a revival. The most recent interpretation of this American classic is Calvin Klein's "Georgica" white ceramic dinnerware, named after Georgica Pond in East Hampton. Photo © Calvin Klein.

Tel. 1-212-292-9000
1-800-294-7978

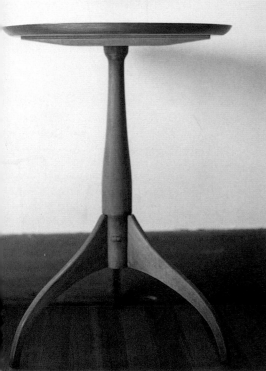

AMERICAN

QUILT

Apart from the bold, graphic charm of these naïve creations, the changes in American quilts across the past two centuries document the nation's development. No wonder then that quilt collecting has developed into a serious pastime. It provides an opportunity to buy a genuine piece of American history. Quilts can realize the kinds of prices at auction that were previously reserved for fine art. Virtually every major American city has at least one dealer, but one particularly selective gallery that features an extraordinary collection of antique quilts belongs to Thomas Woodard and Blanche Greenstein in New York.

Tel. 1-212-988-2906
1-800-332-7847

COLONIAL

RUGS

The American Country aesthetic is derived from the simplicity of the lives of early settlers. Farmers built and painted their own furniture and their wives would weave clothes, linen, and rugs. The crisp plaids, stripes, and checks from their hand-looms could often also be relied on to generate extra income. In time, the weavings of the Pennsylvania Dutch, the Amish, and the Shakers became the popular choice for 19th-century rural homes. Today, the originals are scarce, but these reproductions from Woodard Weave have re-established the classic American woven rug.

Tel. 1-212-988-2906
1-800-332-7847

AUTHENTIC

DETAILS

Renovating an 18th- or 19th-century building can be problematic. A window may be missing, a door damaged beyond repair, or the original interior paneling might have been ripped out. In the past, the search for authentic repairs and replacements could prove frustrating and expensive, but now a company called Architectural Components specializes in alleviating just such difficulties. Using time-honored methods of joinery and construction, they reproduce a wide range of windows, doors, paneling, and moldings that are ideal for use in restoring historic buildings.

Tel. 1-413-367-9441
Fax 1-413-367-9461
Fax 1-212-292-9001

"Every great architect is—necessarily—a great poet.

He must be a great original interpreter of his time, his day, his age."

Frank Lloyd Wright